Kindergarten Puzzles

Level 2

Simple Puzzles, Worksheets, and Activities for Kids

written by

Peter I. Kattan
and
Nicola I. Kattan

PETRA BOOKS
www.PetraBooks.com

Kindergarten Puzzles – Level 2
Simple Puzzles, Worksheets, and Activities for Kids
by Peter I. Kattan and Nicola I. Kattan

The various images appearing in this book were purchased from the Fotolia website at www.fotolia.com . Consequently, the respective authors of these images grant us the right to use these images in this publication royalty free while they retain the copyrights for their work. Thus, we would like to acknowledge their contribution here. The dog and cat images are © Bello from Brazil, the hen image is © Ewe Degiampietro from Germany, the goat image is © piumadaquila from Italy, the bear image is © Alexey Bannykh from Russia, the fax and printer images are © Kamran Akhlag from Pakistan, the computer image is © Elena Svedenco from Moldova, the book image is © Actomic from Germany, and the mouse image is © algabafoto from Spain.

The authors would like to thank Roger White for designing the fonts NationalFirstFontDotted and NationalFirstFont and making them available in the public domain. These font are used on some selected pages of this book. His website address is http://www.rogersfonts.org.uk

Contents

Count the Animals – 1 - -- 5
Count the Animals – 2 - -- 6
Sudoku --- 7
Trace this Number -- 8
Maze --- 8
Draw as Many Shapes as Needed --------------------------------------- 10
What are the Missing Numbers --- 11
Connect the Dots -- 12
Circle Every Occurrence of the Word CAT   -------------------------- 13
Maze --- 14
Count the Triangles -- 15
Sudoku --- 16
Count the Arrows -- 17
Addition --- 18
Color Each Shape -- 19
Find and Circle the Number -- 20
Count then Choose the Correct Number – 1 - -------------------------- 21
Count then Choose the Correct Number – 2 - -------------------------- 22
Trace these Letters -- 23
Draw a Line for the Bear's Journey ----------------------------------- 24
Trace this Number --- 25
Sudoku --- 26
Maze --- 27
Count these Things – 1 - --- 28
Count these Things – 2 - --- 29
Trace these Letters -- 30
Trace this Number --- 31
Count the Steps --- 32
Sudoku --- 33
Maze --- 34
Find the Names of Five Things in the Letter Square? --------------- 35

Contents (Continued)

Count then Choose the Correct Number – 1 - -------------------------- 36
Count then Choose the Correct Number – 2 - -------------------------- 37
Trace this Number --- 38
Sudoku --- 39
Secret Words --- 40
Maze --- 41
Addition --- 42
Kakuro --- 43
Count then Chose the Correct Number ------------------------------- 44
Connect the Dots --- 45
Sudoku --- 46
Subtraction -- 47
Maze --- 48
Trace this Number -- 49
Count the Squares -- 50
Circle Every Occurrence of the Word DOG -------------------------- 51
Sudoku --- 52
Count the Shapes --- 53
Maze --- 54
Find the Names of Five Animals in the Letter Square? -------------- 55
Find and Circle the Number --------------------------------------- 56
Count the Circles -- 57
Trace this Number -- 58
Subtraction -- 59
Secret Words --- 60
Kakuro --- 61

Count the Animals

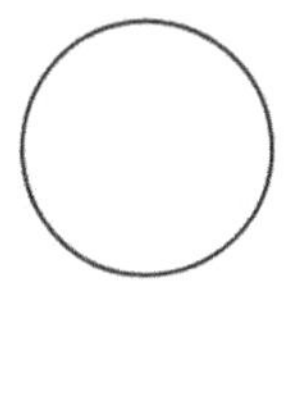

Count the Animals

Sudoku
Fill the blanks with the numbers 1,2,3,4 such that

01   Each row has the four numbers 1,2,3,4 appearing just once.

02   Each Column has the four numbers 1,2,3,4 appearing just once.

03   Each 2x2 block has the four numbers 1,2,3,4 appearing just once.

1		2	4
			3
	1		
4	2	3	

Trace these Numbers

6   6   6   6   6

7   7   7   7   7

8   8   8   8   8

9   9   9   9   9

10   10   10   10   10

Maze

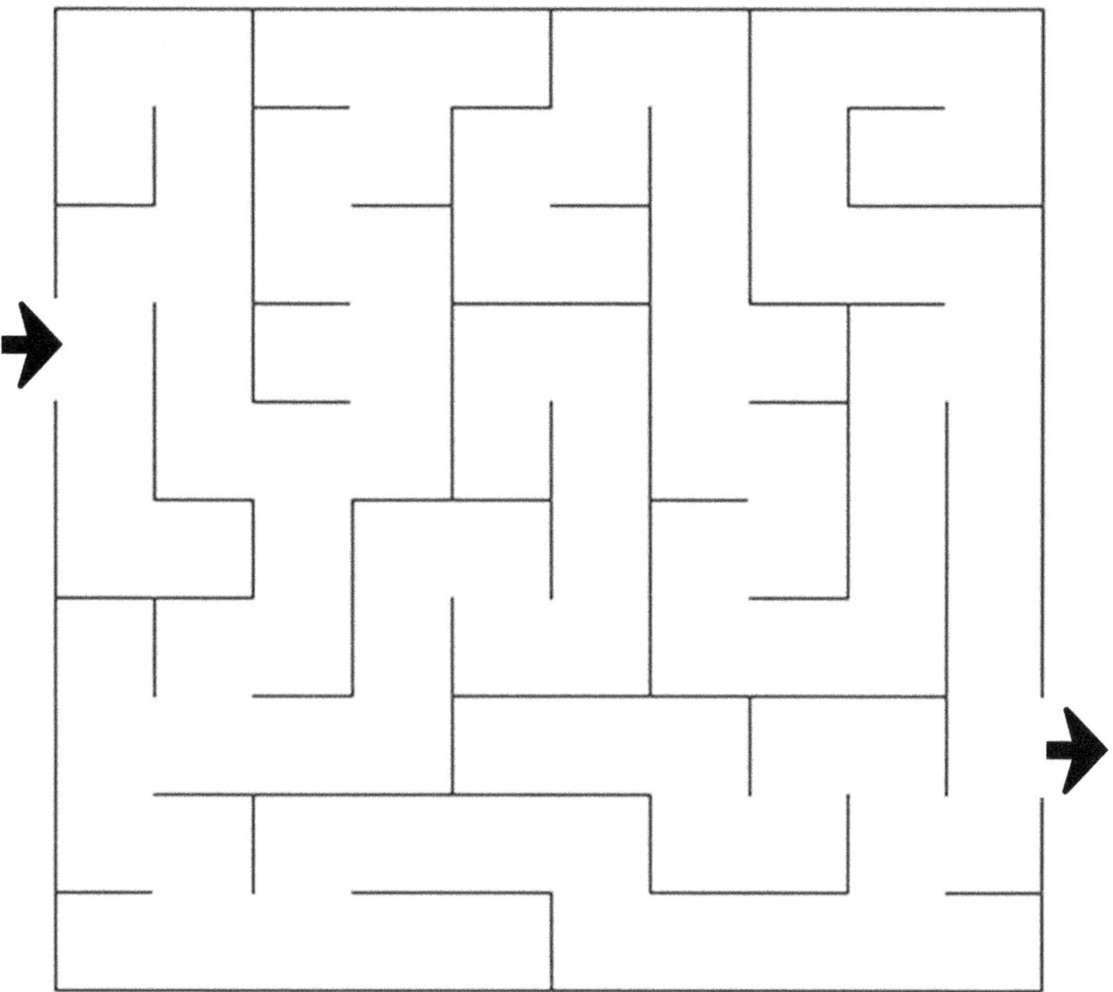

Draw as Many Shapes as Needed

7	10	8	6	9
▢	◯	△	★	◇

What are the Missing Numbers

6		8		10

	7		9	10

6	7		9	

6		8	9	

Connect the Dots

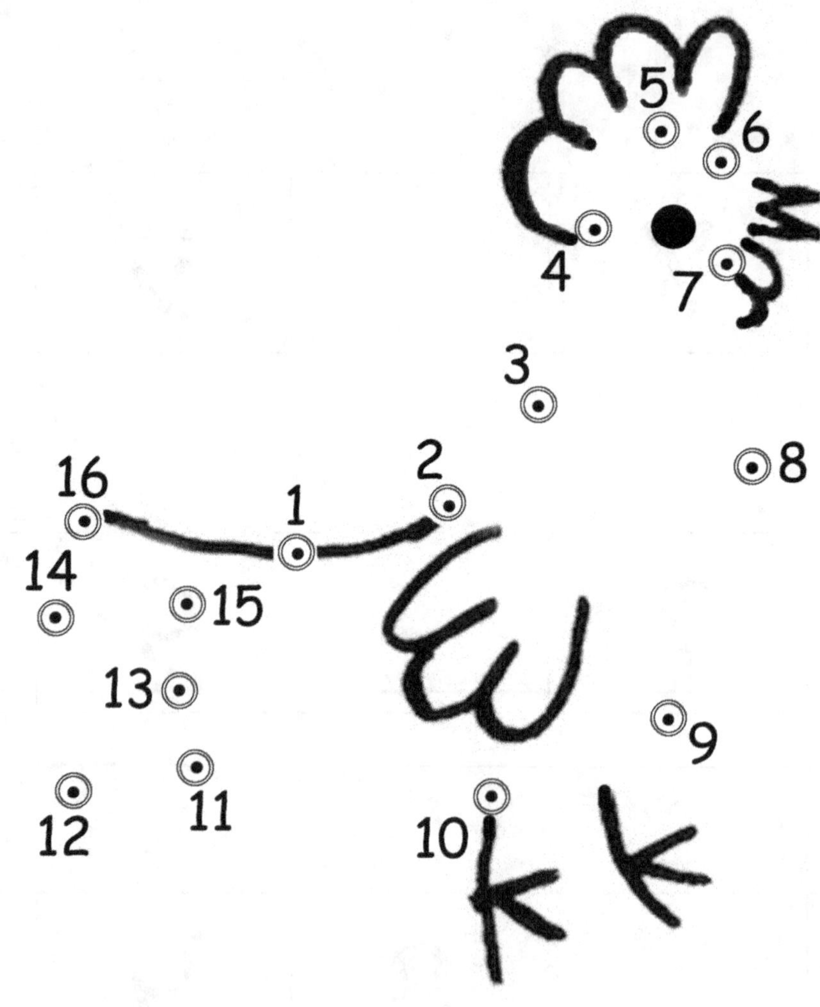

Circle Every Occurrence of the Word CAT

RAT	CAT	DOG	MOON
BOY	RAT	MAN	CAT
CAT	SUN	CAT	MAN
MOON	BOY	DOG	MAN
CAT	BOY	RAT	SUN
MAN	MOON	CAT	BOY

How many times CAT occurs? _________

Maze

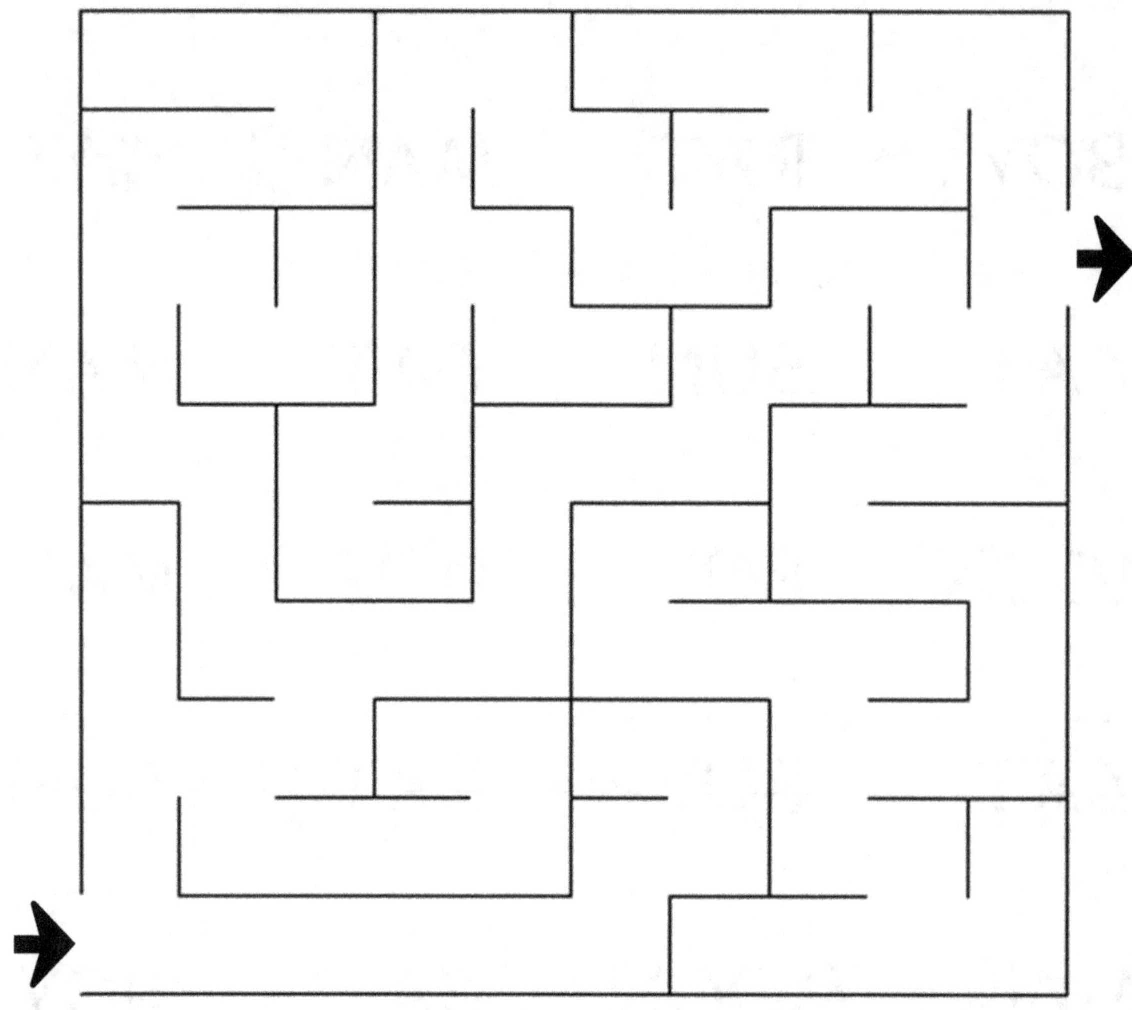

Count the Triangles

Number of Triangles is ? ______

Sudoku
Fill the blanks with the numbers 1,2,3,4 such that

01   Each row has the four numbers 1,2,3,4 appearing just once.

02   Each Column has the four numbers 1,2,3,4 appearing just once.

03   Each 2x2 block has the four numbers 1,2,3,4 appearing just once.

3	2		4
4	1		
		2	
2			1

Count the Arrows

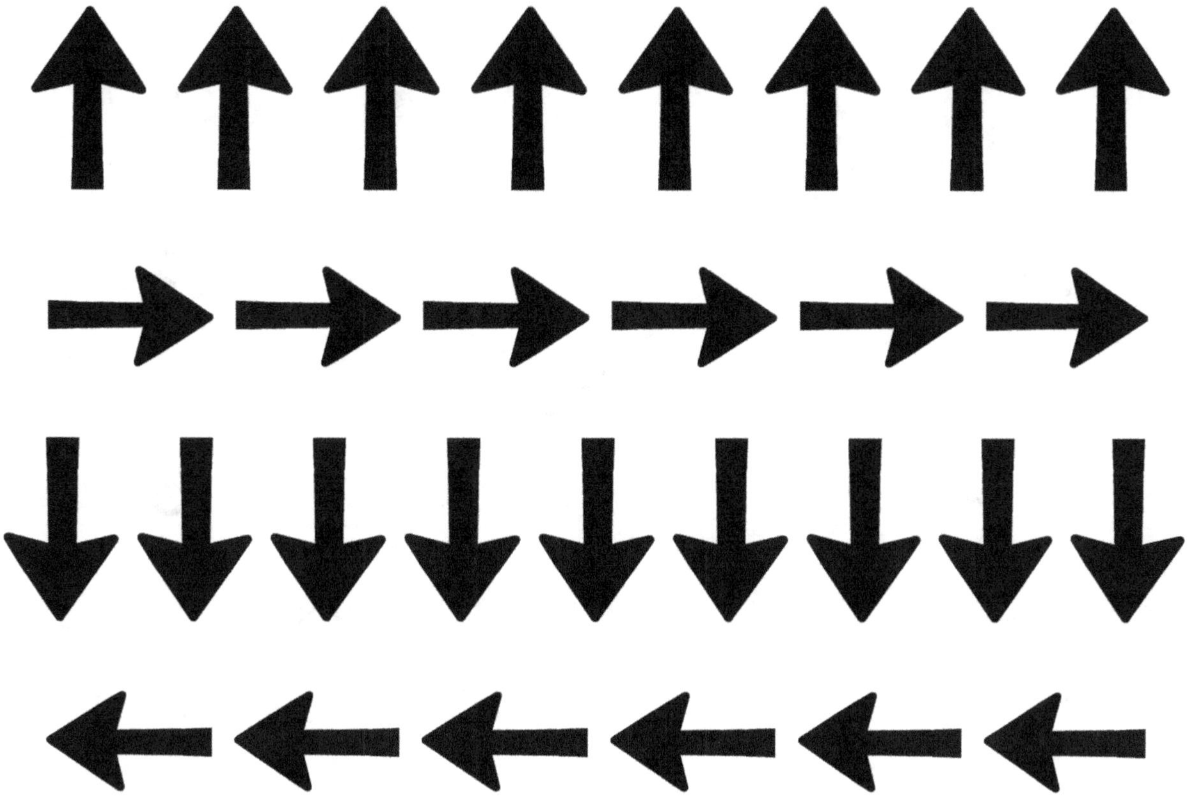

up   (8)   down   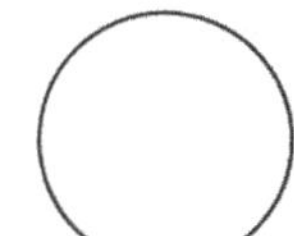

right   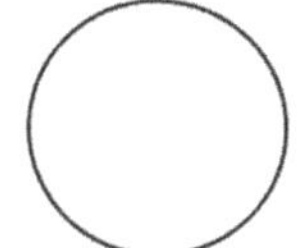   left   ( )

Addition

2 + 6   7

4 + 1   2

5 + 2   3

3 + 3   8

2 + 0   5

1 + 2   4

3 + 1   6

Color Each Shape, then Draw the Shape in the Corresponding Box in the Right Column

Red (Number 8)	6
Blue (Number 6)	7
Green (Number 9)	8
Yellow (Number 7)	9
Orange (Number 10)	10

Find and Circle the Number 6

5	2	6	7	8	1	0
2	4	5	7	6	5	3
6	5	1	2	5	6	8

Find and Circle the Number 7

2	7	9	8	4	3	6
7	8	9	1	2	3	7
7	0	1	2	7	4	3

Find and Circle the Number 8

1	3	8	6	7	8	5
5	8	3	8	6	7	8
8	1	2	3	4	8	1

Count then Choose the Correct Number

7　　（6）　　8

8　　9　　10

8　　9　　10

Count then Choose the Correct Number

6   7   8

7   8   9

8   9   10

Trace these Letters

O   O   O   O   O

P   P   P   P   P

Q   Q   Q   Q   Q

R   R   R   R   R

S   S   S   S   S

T   T   T   T   T

The Bear Wants to Go Around the Numbers
Draw a Line for its Journey

Trace this Number

6	6	6	6	6	6
6	6	6	6		
6	6				

Sudoku
Fill the blanks with the numbers 1,2,3,4 such that

01   Each row has the four numbers 1,2,3,4 appearing just once.

02   Each Column has the four numbers 1,2,3,4 appearing just once.

03   Each 2x2 block has the four numbers 1,2,3,4 appearing just once.

4		3	2
	3		1
		1	
1		2	

Maze

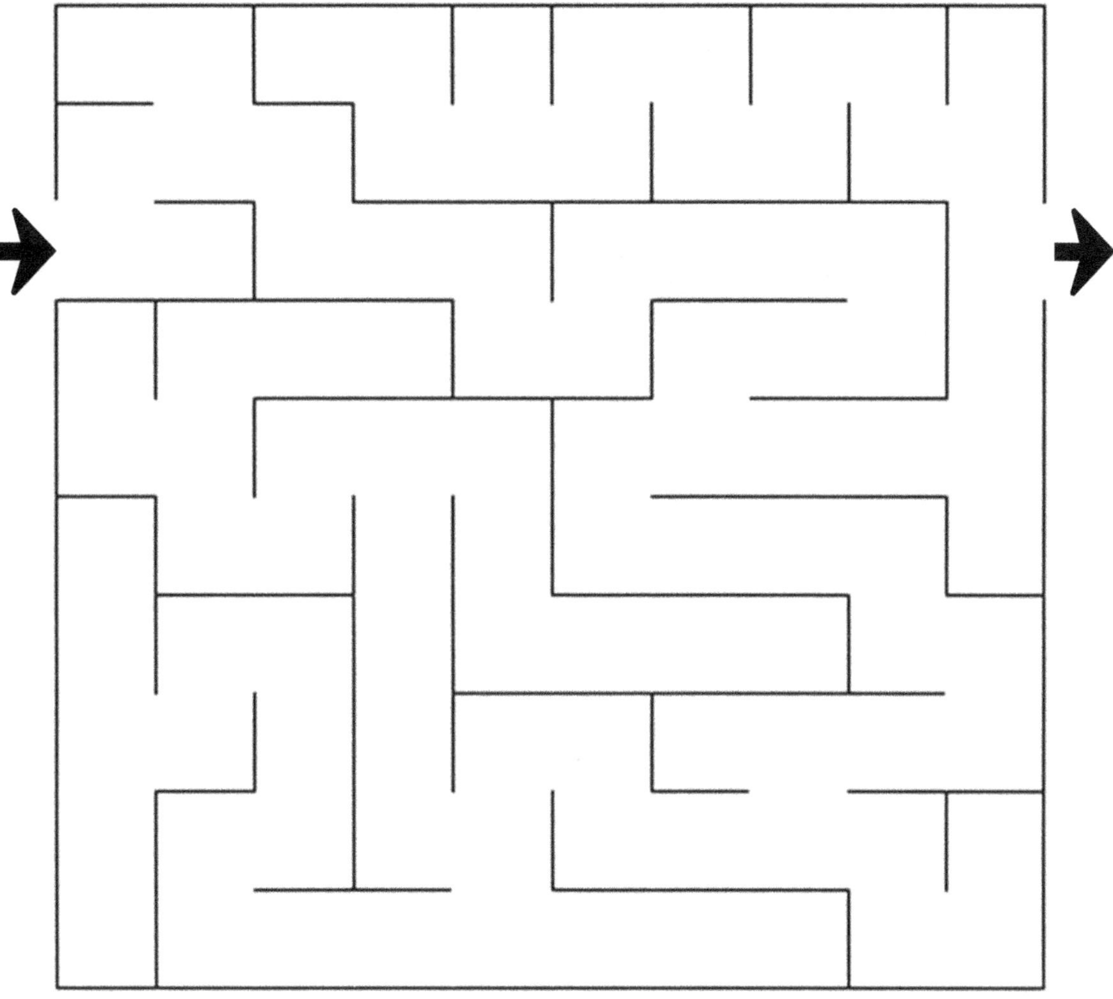

Count these Things

10

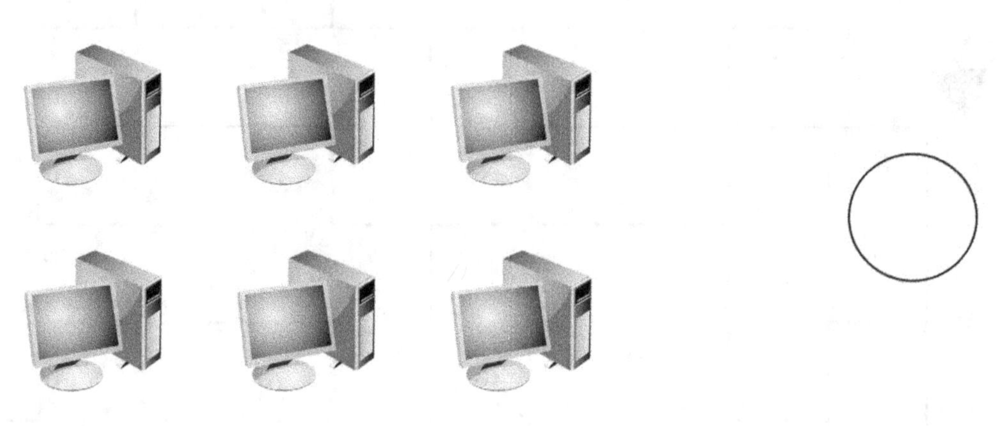

Count these Things

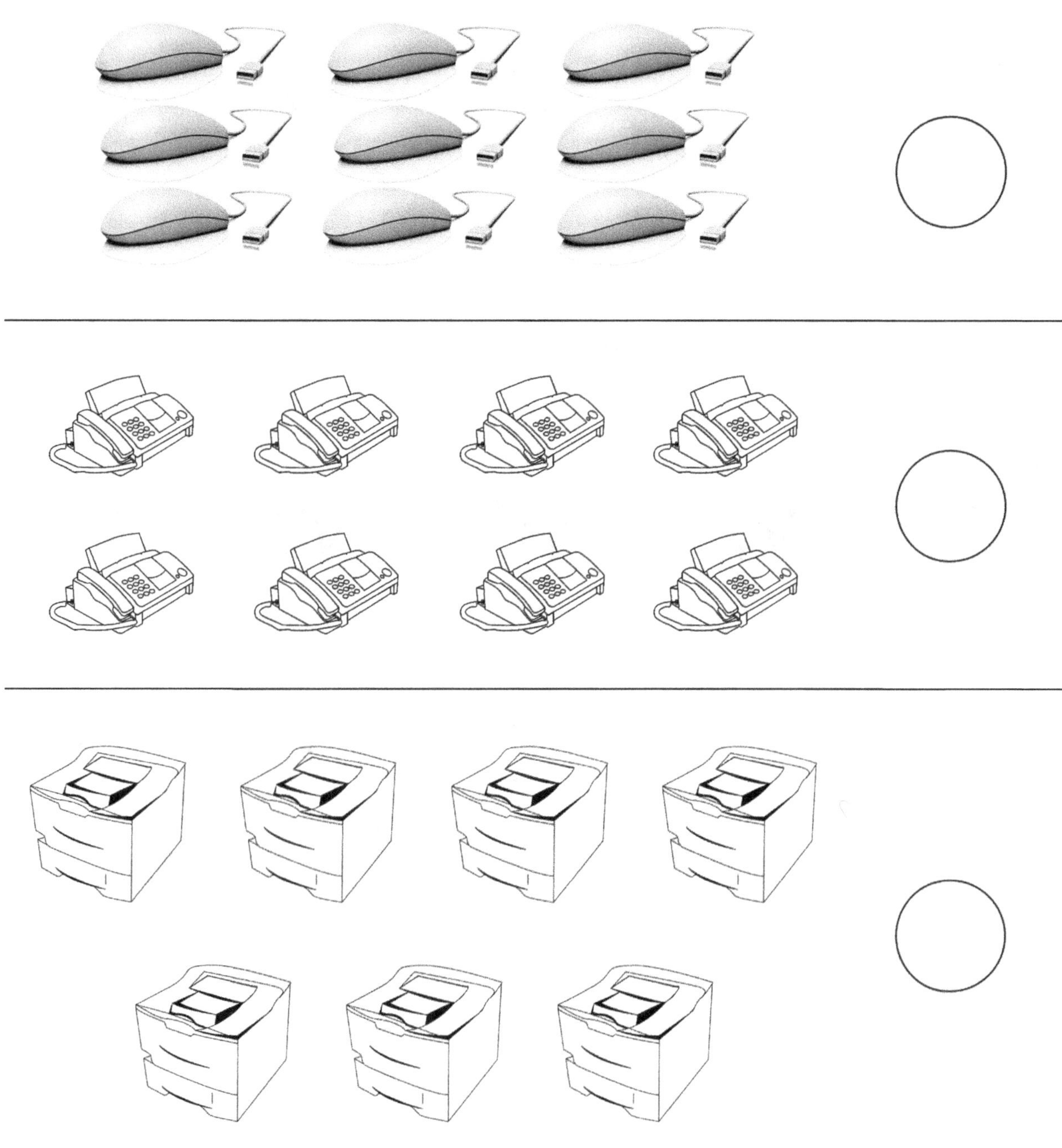

Trace these Letters

U   U   U   U   U

V   V   V   V   V

W   W   W   W   W

X   X   X   X   X

Y   Y   Y   Y   Y

Z   Z   Z   Z   Z

Trace this Number

7	7	7	7	7	7
7	7	7	7		
7	7				

Count the Steps

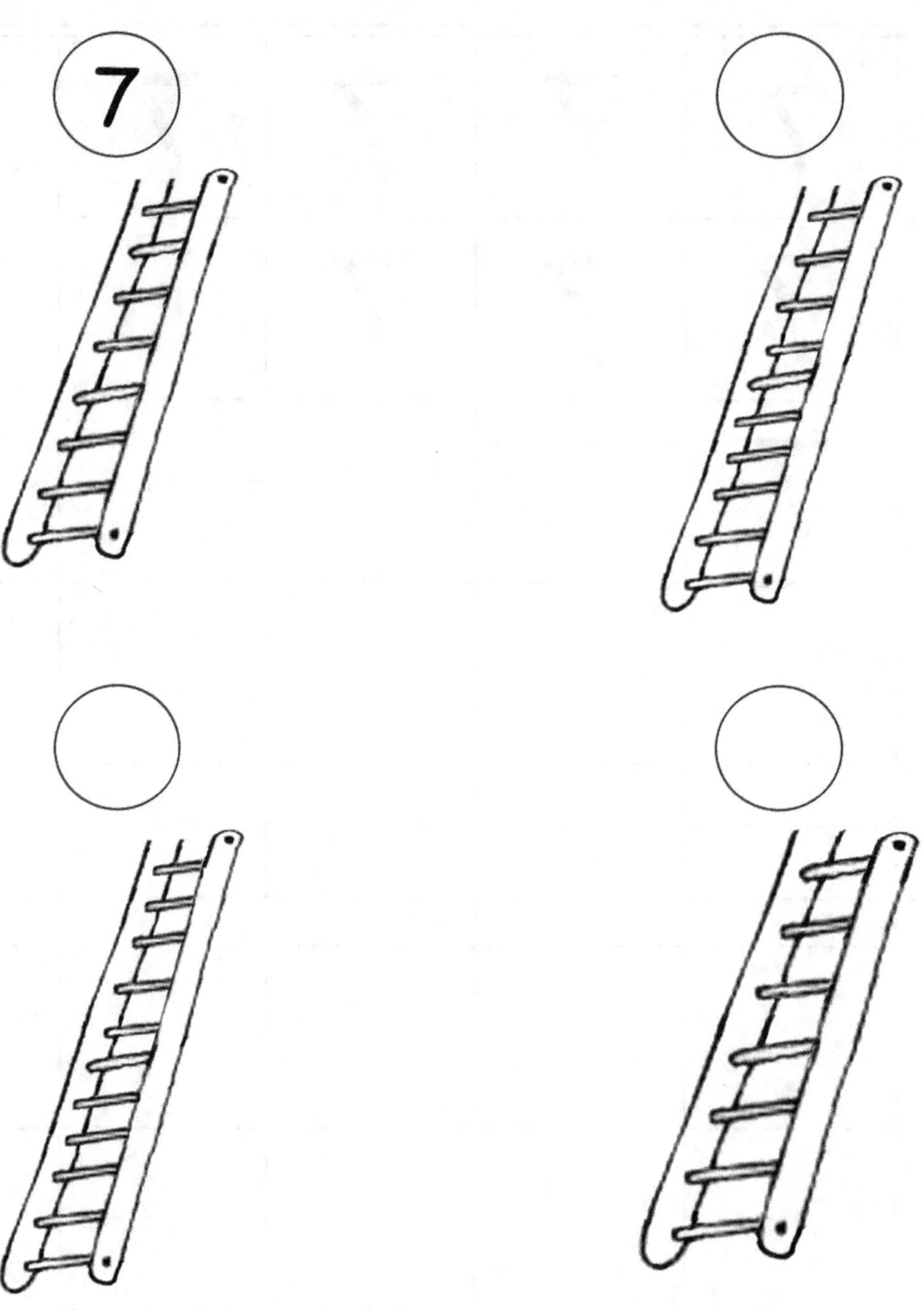

Sudoku
Fill the blanks with the numbers 1,2,3,4 such that

01 Each row has the four numbers 1,2,3,4 appearing just once.

02 Each Column has the four numbers 1,2,3,4 appearing just once.

03 Each 2x2 block has the four numbers 1,2,3,4 appearing just once.

	3	4	1
	1		
	4	3	2
			4

Maze

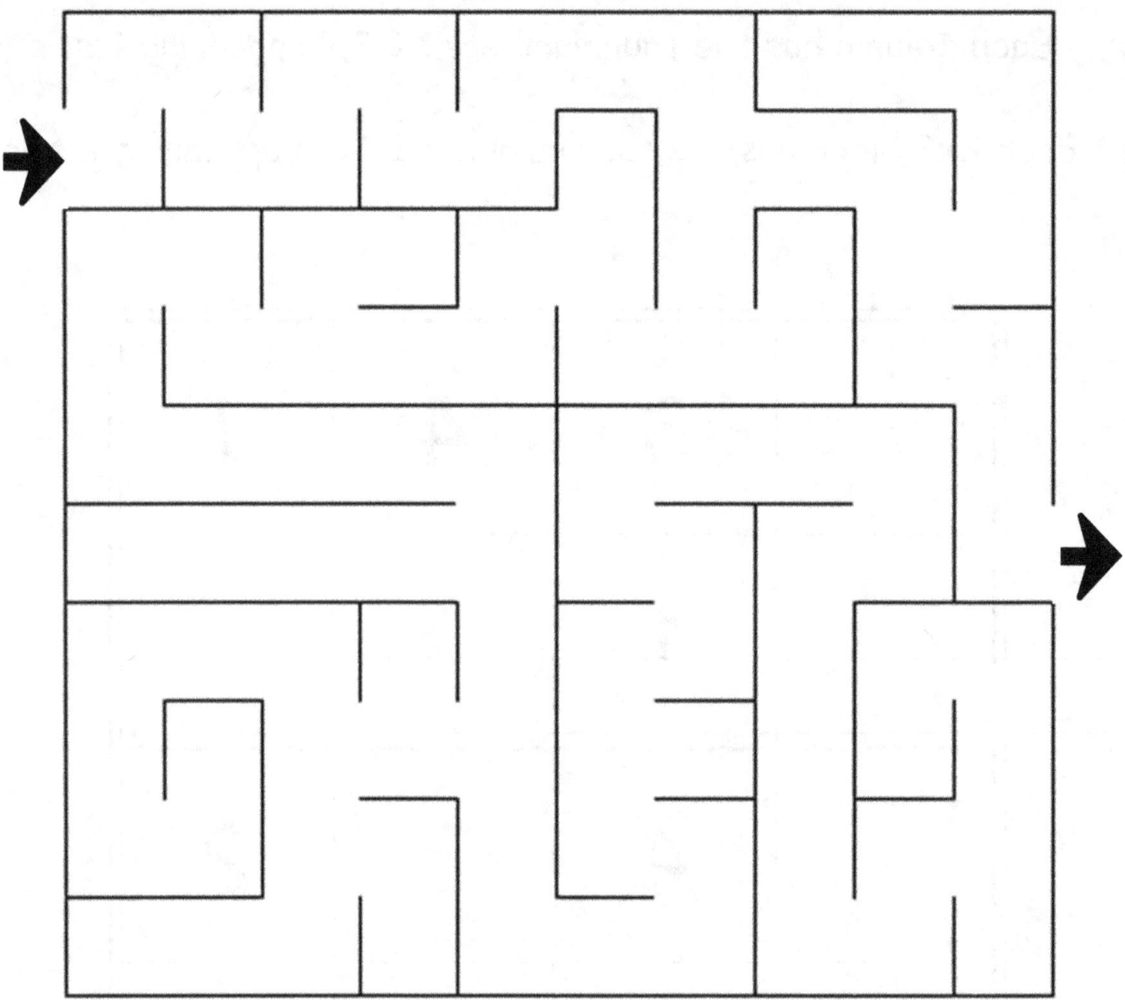

Find the Names of Five Things in the Letter Square?

FAX, MOUSE, BOOK, KEY, PEN

M	A	B	C	D	K
O	E	F	A	X	E
U	F	G	H	I	Y
S	J	K	M	N	O
E	L	B	O	O	K
P	P	E	N	Q	R

Colors the Names:

FAX	→	YELLOW
MOUSE	→	GREEN
BOOK	→	BLUE
KEY	→	ORANGE
PEN	→	RED

Count then Choose the Correct Number

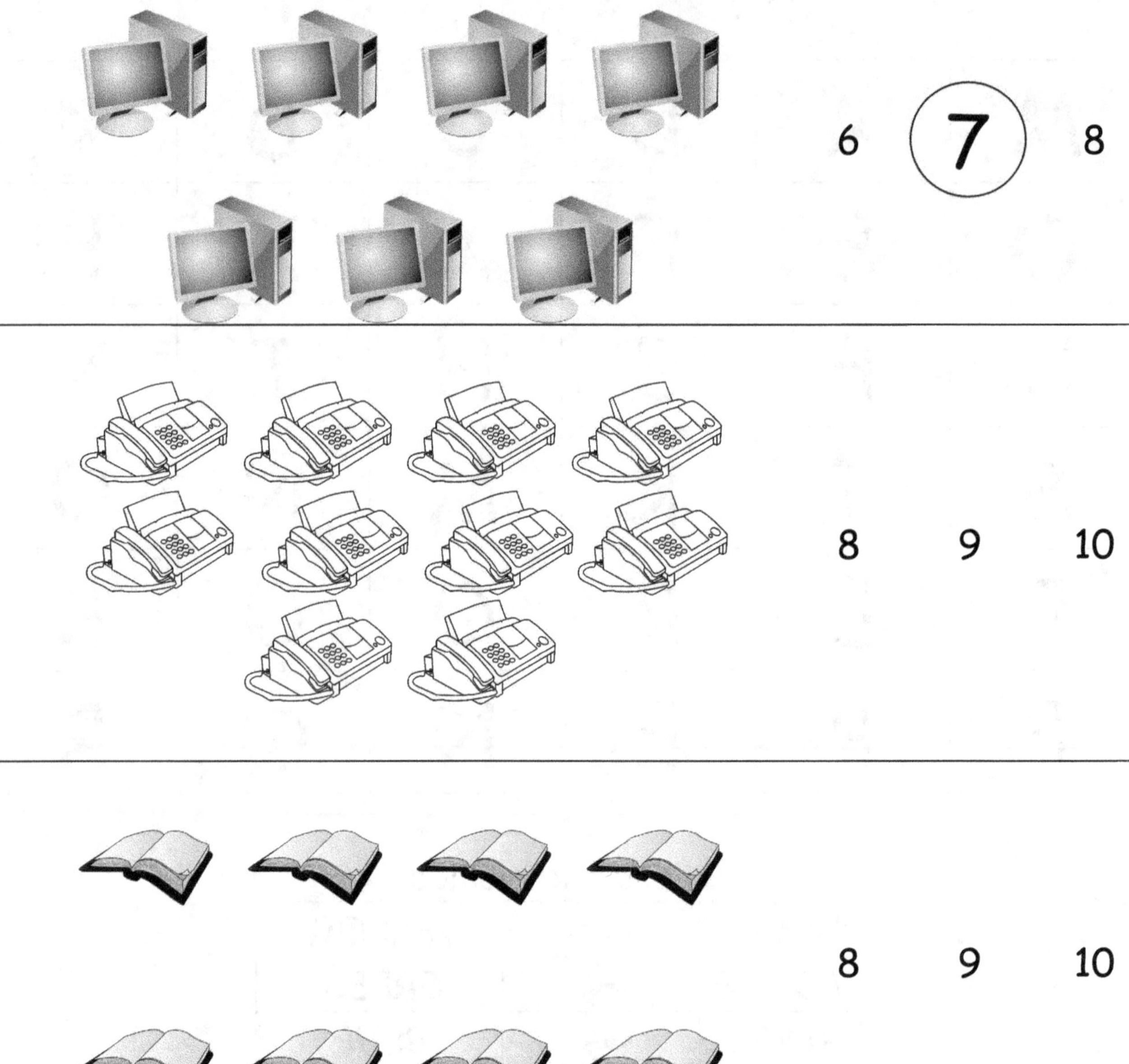

6　(7)　8

8　9　10

8　9　10

Count then Choose the Correct Number

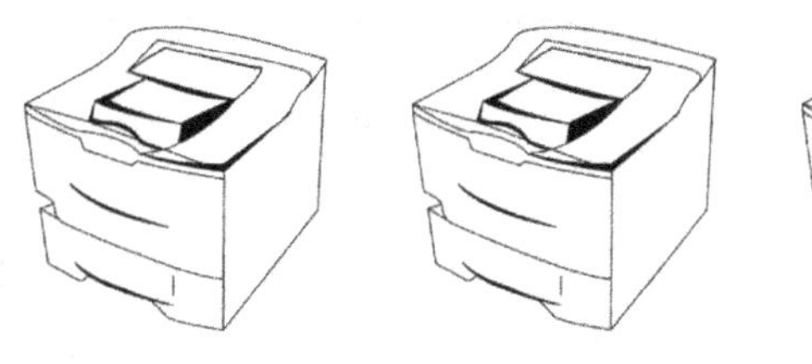

5   6   7

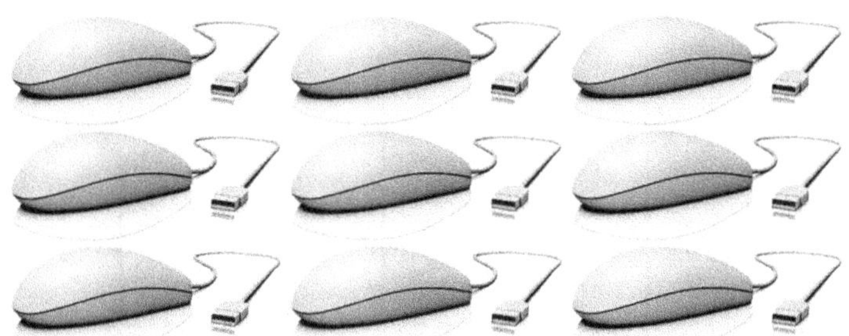

8   9   10

7   6   8

Trace this Number

8	8	8	8	8	8
8	8	8	8		
8	8				

Sudoku
Fill the blanks with the numbers 1,2,3,4 such that

01 Each row has the four numbers 1,2,3,4 appearing just once.

02 Each Column has the four numbers 1,2,3,4 appearing just once.

03 Each 2x2 block has the four numbers 1,2,3,4 appearing just once.

3	4	1	
		4	
4		2	
	2		4

Secret Words

2 - 5 - 1 - 18 =
2 → B   5 → E   1 → A   18 → R
2 - 5 - 1 - 18 = BEAR

1	A
2	B
3	C
4	D
5	E
6	F
7	G

14	N
15	O
16	P
17	Q
18	R
19	S
20	T

What are the Secret Words hidden by the following number codes:

3 - 1 - 20 =
4 - 15 - 7 =
7 - 15 - 1 - 20 =
8 - 5 - 14 =
6 - 1 - 24 =
13 - 15 - 21 - 19 - 5 =
2 - 15 - 15 - 11 =

8	H
9	I
10	J
11	K
12	L
13	M

21	U
22	V
23	W
24	X
25	Y
26	Z

Maze

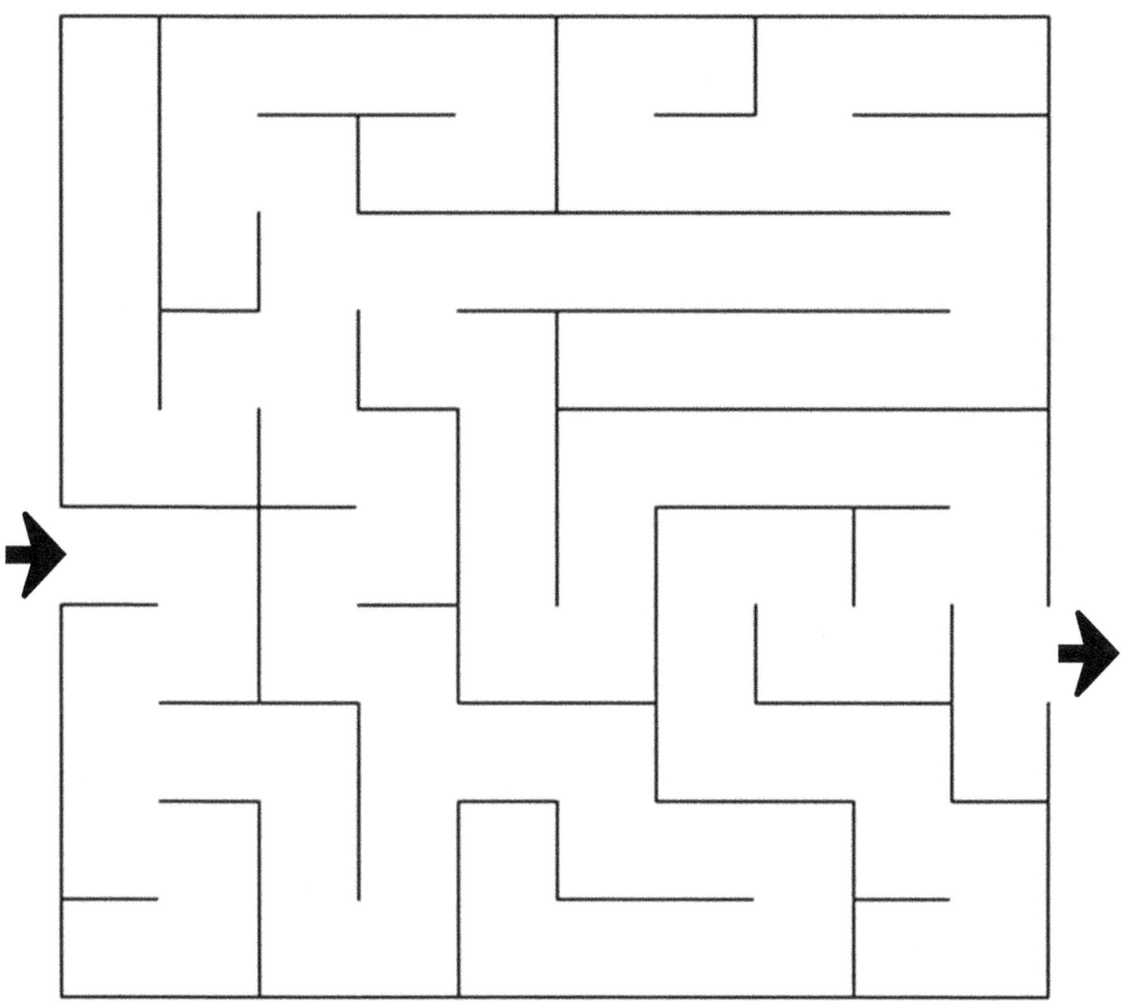

Addition

4 + 5	4
3 + 3	5
2 + 3	7
6 + 2	9
4 + 0	3
2 + 5	6
1 + 2	8

Kindergarten Puzzles – Level 2

Kakuro

Fill the blank cells with some of the numbers 1 - 9 such that the sum of the numbers in each set of consecutive white cells (horizontal or vertical) is the number appearing to the left of a set or above a set. No number may appear more than once in any consecutive set of numbers.

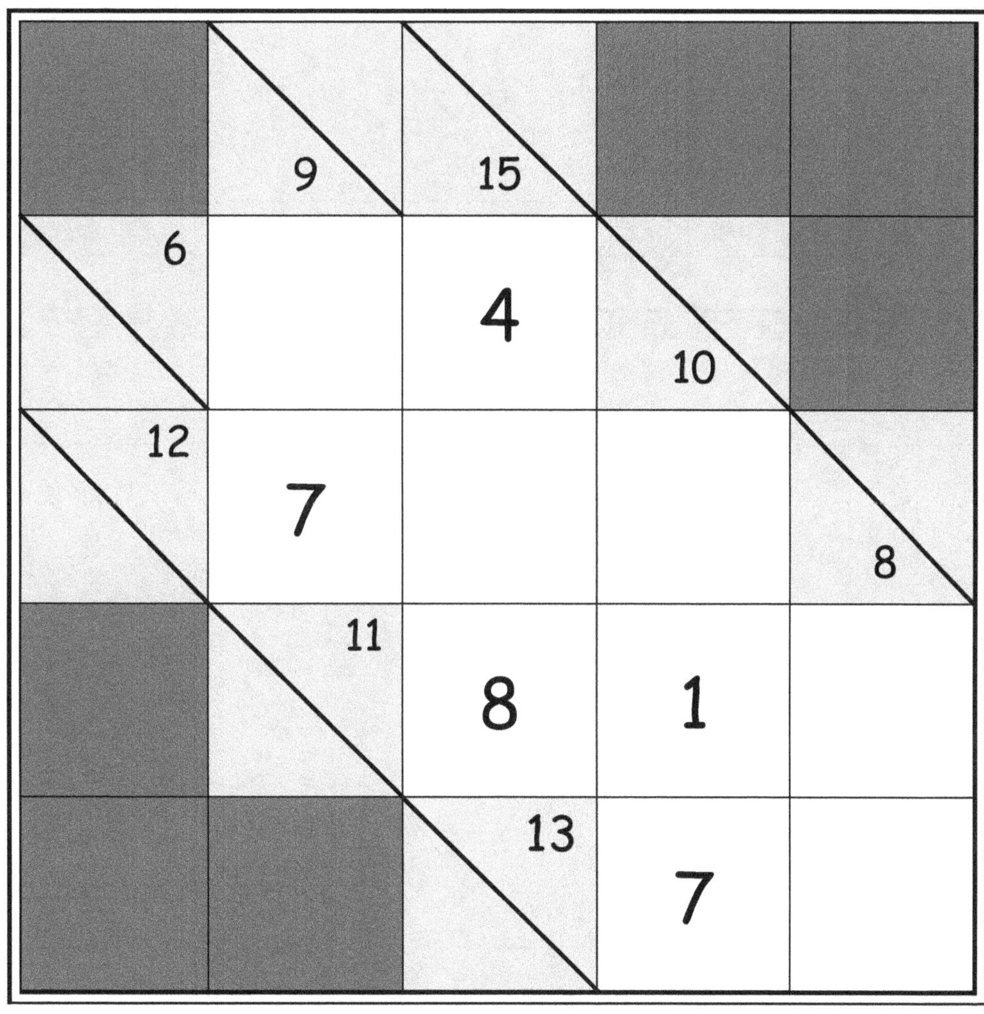

Count then Chose the Correct Number

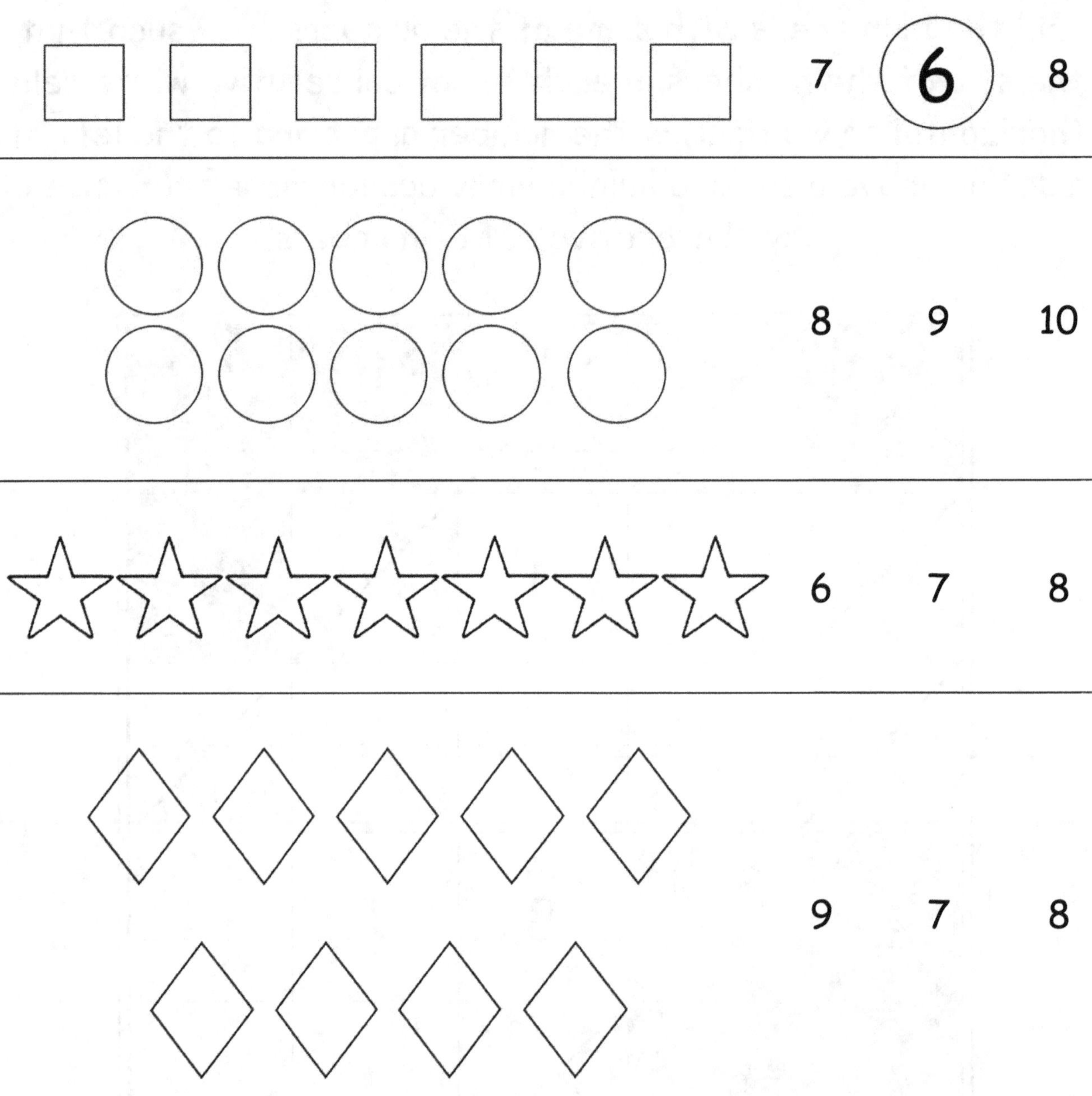

7   Ⓐ**6**   8

8   9   10

6   7   8

9   7   8

Connect the Dots

Sudoku
Fill the blanks with the numbers 1,2,3,4 such that

01   Each row has the four numbers 1,2,3,4 appearing just once.

02   Each Column has the four numbers 1,2,3,4 appearing just once.

03   Each 2x2 block has the four numbers 1,2,3,4 appearing just once.

		1	
1			3
4	3	2	
2	1		

Subtraction

4 - 1	1
3 - 2	5
5 - 3	7
7 - 2	3
5 - 1	2
9 - 3	4
7 - 0	6

Maze

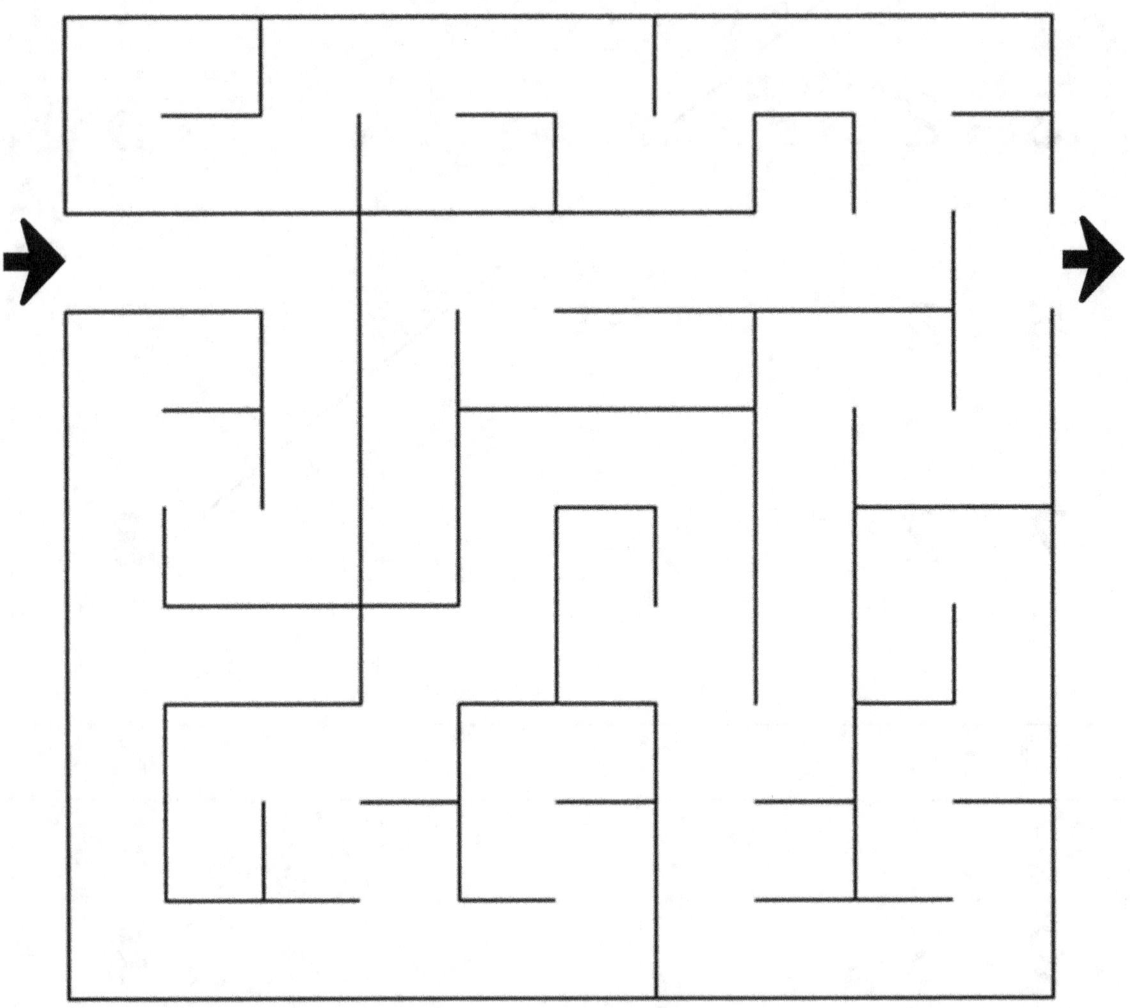

Trace this Number

9	9	9	9	9	9
9	9	9	9		
9	9				

Count the Squares

Number of Squares is ? _________

Circle Every Occurrence of the Word DOG

RAT	CAT	DOG	MOON
DOG	MAN	BOY	CAT
MAN	RAT	DOG	MOON
BOY	MAN	DOG	CAT
MAN	DOG	BOY	DOG
DOG	BOY	MAN	MOON

How many times DOG occurs? ________

Sudoku

Fill the blanks with the numbers 1,2,3,4 such that

01   Each row has the four numbers 1,2,3,4 appearing just once.

02   Each Column has the four numbers 1,2,3,4 appearing just once.

03   Each 2x2 block has the four numbers 1,2,3,4 appearing just once.

	3	2	
	2		3
3			
	4	3	1

Count the Shapes

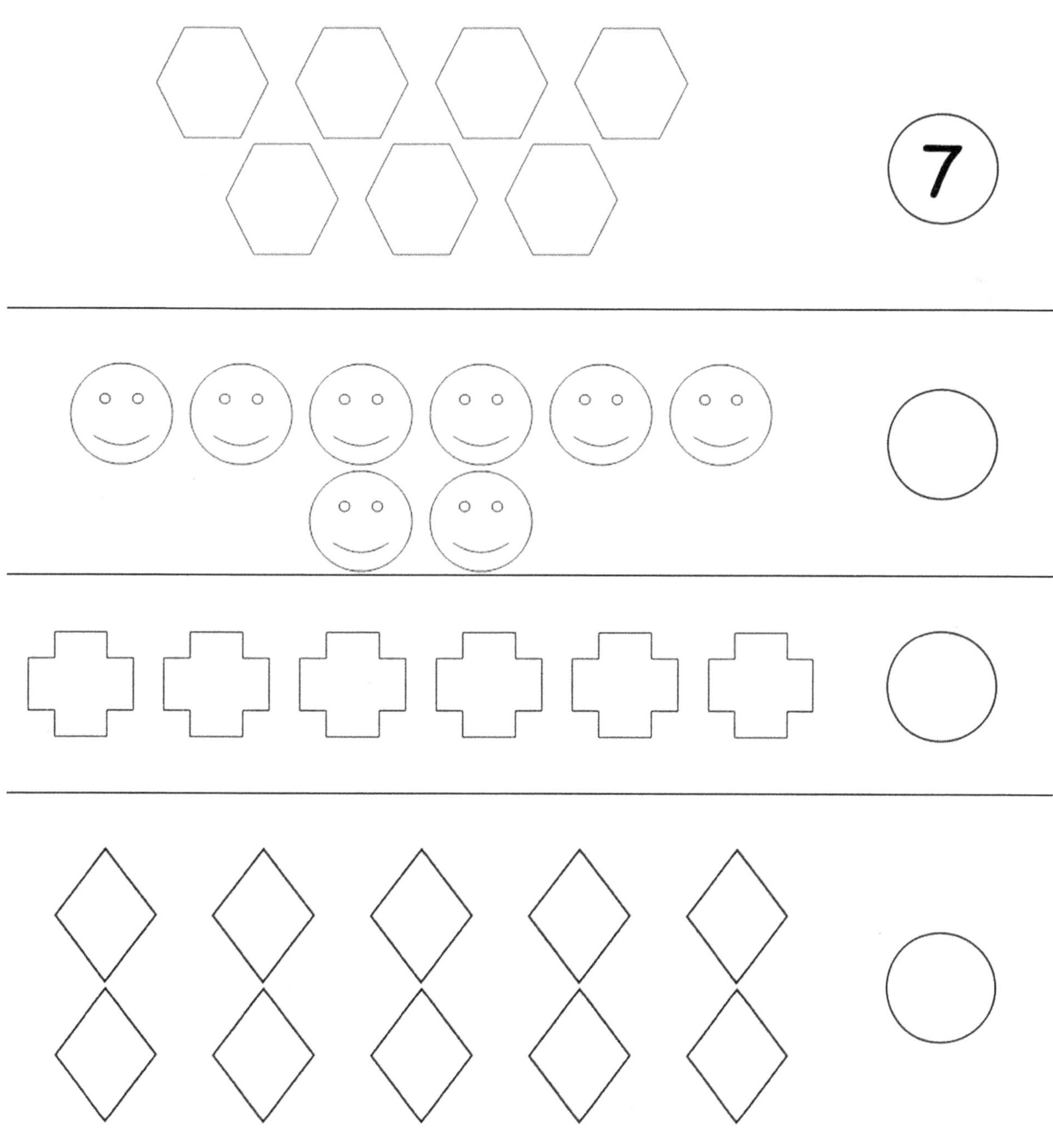

Maze

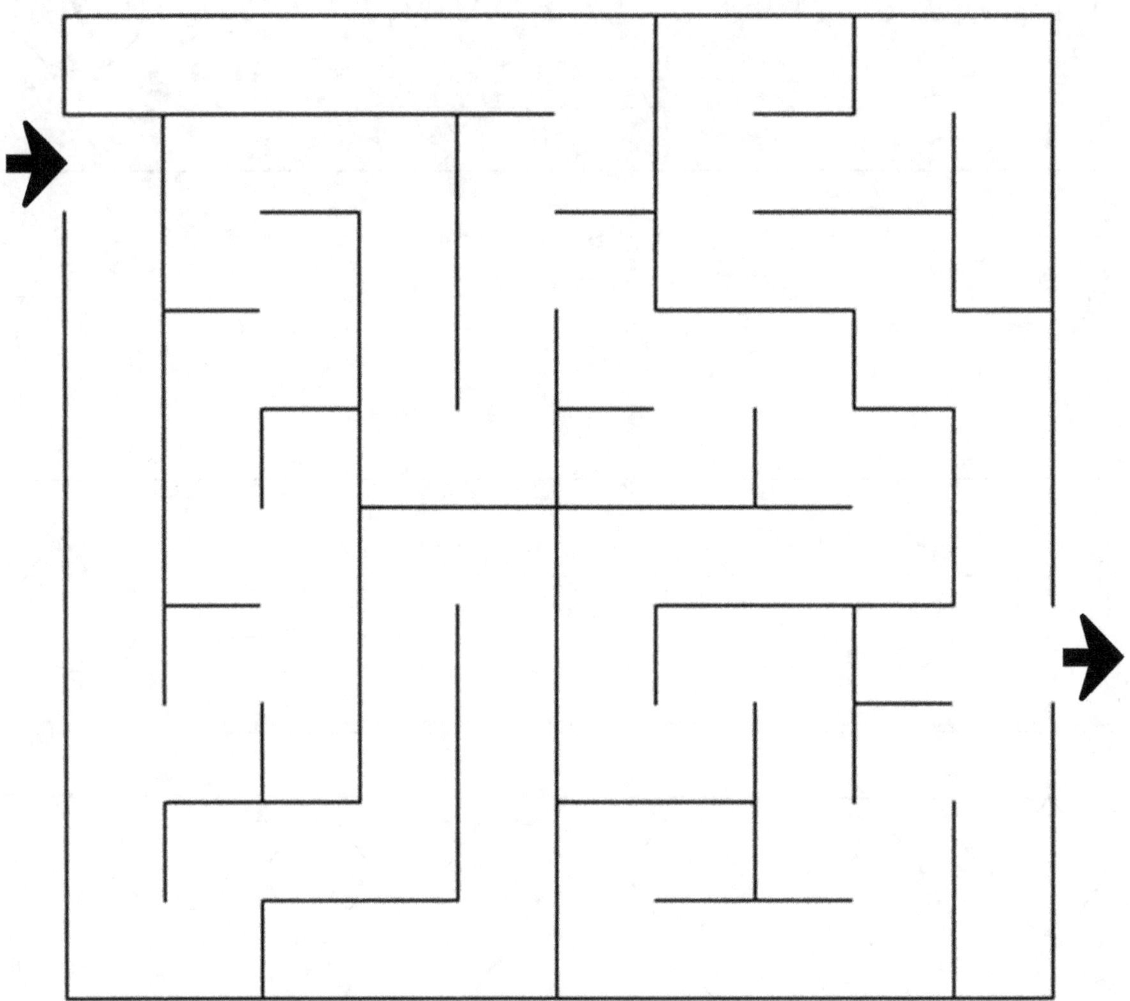

Find the Names of Five Animals in the Letter Square?

BEAR, CAT, DOG, GOAT, HEN

A	B	C	O	R	M
U	B	E	A	R	N
C	V	X	H	E	N
A	R	S	T	D	U
T	P	W	Y	O	Z
G	O	A	T	G	F

Colors the Names:

BEAR	→	RED
CAT	→	YELLOW
DOG	→	BLUE
GOAT	→	GREEN
HEN	→	ORANGE

Find and Circle the Number 9

1	9	10	2	3	6	9
8	1	9	3	4	7	8
9	3	2	1	4	9	7
1	3	9	1	2	9	4

Find and Circle the Number 10

10	2	1	3	9	10	8
7	8	10	2	7	8	10
2	3	1	4	10	1	2
7	8	9	10	1	2	3

Count the Circles

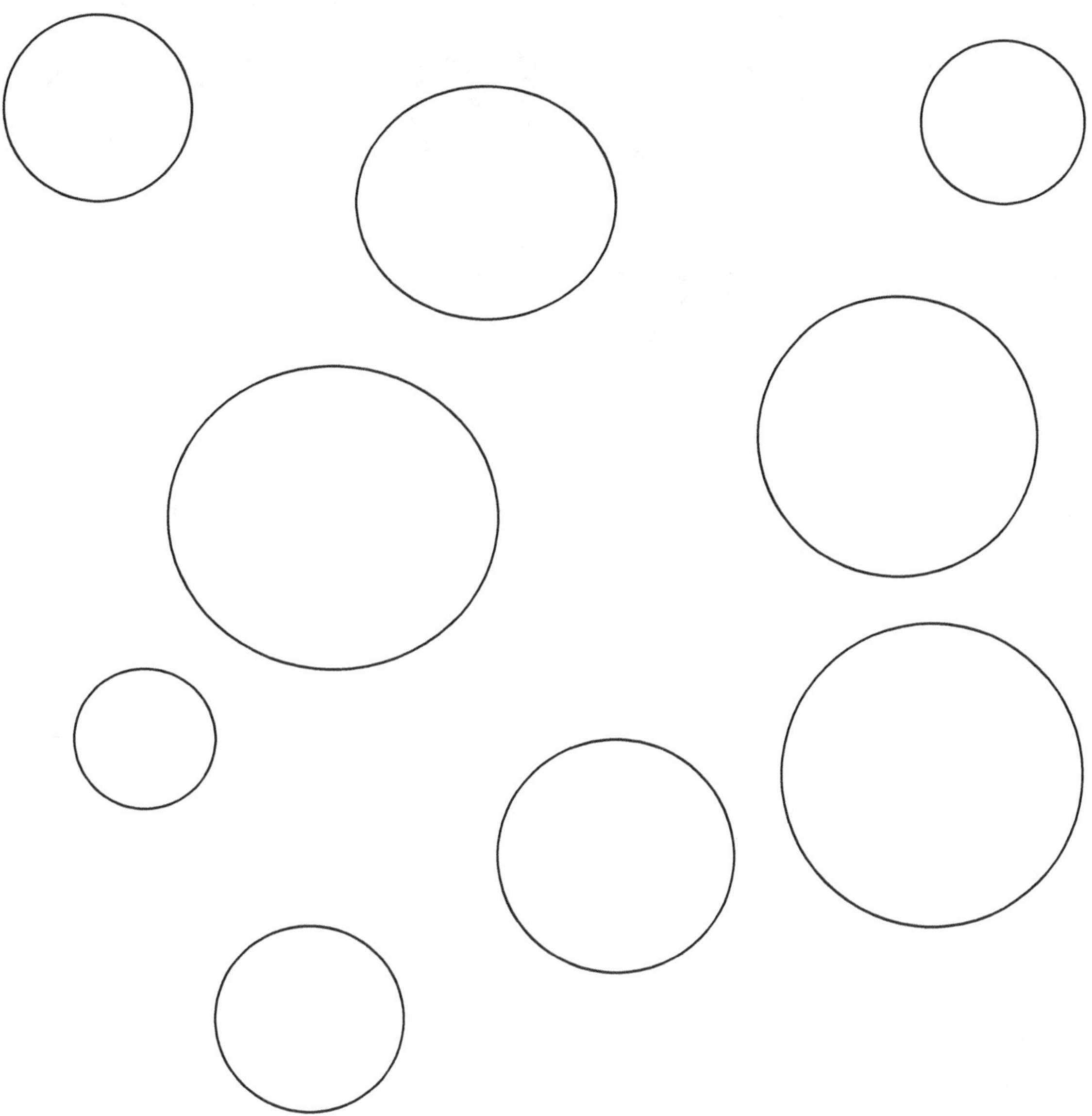

Number of Circles is ? ___________

Trace this Number

10	10	10	10	10	10
10	10	10	10		
10	10				

Subtraction

3 - 1	3
4 - 0	6
5 - 2	7
9 - 3	8
7 - 2	4
9 - 2	2
8 - 0	5

Secret Words

18 – 5 – 4 =
18 ➜ R
5 ➜ E
4 ➜ D
18 – 5 – 4 = RED

1	A
2	B
3	C
4	D
5	E
6	F
7	G

14	N
15	O
16	P
17	Q
18	R
19	S
20	T

What are the Secret Words hidden by the following number codes:

2 – 12 – 21 – 5 =
7 – 18 – 5 – 5 – 14 =
15 – 18 – 1 – 14 – 7 – 5 =
25 – 5 – 12 – 12 – 15 – 23 =
2 – 12 – 1 – 3 – 11 =

8	H
9	I
10	J
11	K
12	L
13	M

21	U
22	V
23	W
24	X
25	Y
26	Z

Kakuro

Fill the blank cells with some of the numbers 1 - 9 such that the sum of the numbers in each set of consecutive white cells (horizontal or vertical) is the number appearing to the left of a set or above a set. No number may appear more than once in any consecutive set of numbers.

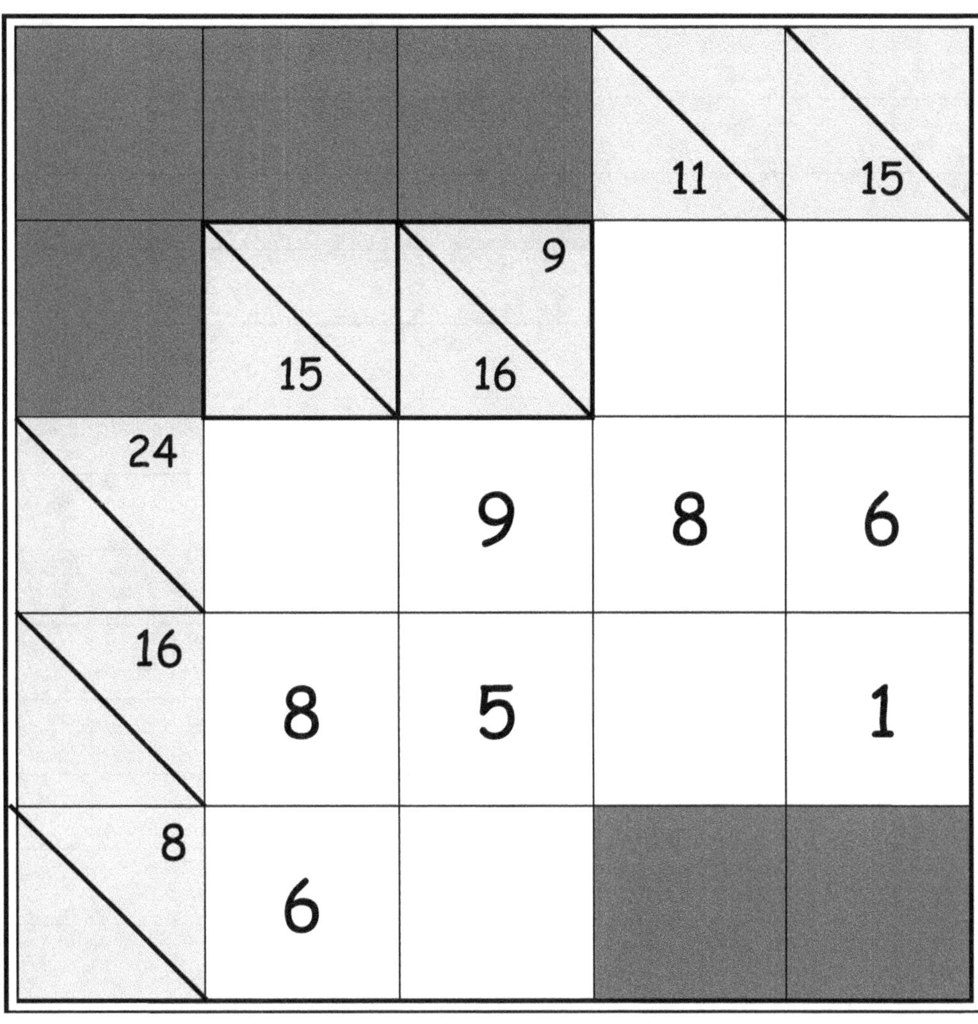

Name:

Age:

Notes

Kindergarten Puzzles – Level 1
Simple Puzzles, Worksheets, and Activities for Kids

Check the companion book containing Level 1 puzzles that include mazes, Sudoku, counting, matching, letter puzzles, and shape puzzles.

Also Available by the Same Authors:

Kindergarten Sudoku
4x4 Sudoku Puzzles for Kids

More Kindergarten Sudoku
4x4 Classic Sudoku Puzzles for Kids

The Big Book of Kindergarten Sudoku
4x4 Sudoku Puzzles for Kids

Beyond Kindergarten Sudoku
6x6 Sudoku Puzzles for Kids

www.ingramcontent.com/pod-product-compliance
Lightning Source LLC
Chambersburg PA
CBHW080003180726
48002CB00020B/2937